better together*

*This book is best read together, grownup and kid.

 akidsco.com

a kids book about

a kids book about AGEISM

by the Connecticut Age Well Collaborative

a kids book about

Text and design copyright © 2024
by A Kids Book About, Inc.

Copyright is good! It ensures that work like this can exist, and more work in the future can be created.

All rights reserved. No part of this publication may be reproduced, distributed, or transmitted in any form or by any means, including photocopying, recording, other electronic or mechanical methods, without the prior written permission of the publisher, except in the case of brief quotations embodied in critical reviews and certain other noncommercial uses permitted by copyright law. For permission requests, write to the publisher.

A Kids Book About, Kids Are Ready, and the colophon 'a' are trademarks of A Kids Book About, Inc.

Printed in the United States of America.

A Kids Book About books are available online: *akidsco.com*

To share your stories, ask questions, or inquire about bulk purchases (schools, libraries, and nonprofits), please use the following email address: *hello@akidsco.com*

Print ISBN: 979-8-89281-036-4
Ebook ISBN: 979-8-89281-037-1

Designed by Jelani Memory
Edited by Emma Wolf

Contributors to this book include Lisa Rampulla Bress, Christina Gray, Karen Green, Teresa Gregory Hines, Lesley Holford, Cynthia Hyland, Alyssa Norwood, and Julia Evans Starr.

To anyone who has ever felt invisible—we see and celebrate you and your ageless essence.

To you, our readers—thank you for your part in shaping a world in which we all truly belong, regardless of age or ability.

To Ashton Applewhite, Tracey Gendron, Becca Levy, Janine Vanderburg, and the ever-growing number of change agents working to disrupt ageism—thank you for shining your light.

Intro

We're all lucky to be alive, to be aging. We're living longer and healthier lives than at any other time in human history. This means that our minds and bodies will change over time as we grow older. Living is aging!

This book exists to tell a more complete story of aging. Aging is something we all do—our loved ones, our community members, our current and future selves. As a society, we often wrongly believe that being young, productive, efficient, self-reliant, and physically strong are always better than any alternatives. Those false ideas can make us fear and dislike growing older, or see it as something other people do, but not us. But there's so much more to the story!

Growing older—like anything worthwhile in life—can be challenging sometimes. And it provides the opportunity to celebrate new kinds of strength.

Hi! The team writing this book is a group of people growing older, just like you— and everyone else.

Growing older, or aging, is the normal process of our minds and bodies changing over time.

Every person ages!

Aging is a baby getting bigger.

Aging is adding candles to your birthday cake.

Aging is learning new skills.

Aging is growing up.

Aging is collecting stories and experiences about yourself and others.

Aging is about growing much older.

Aging is beautiful.

And, aging is important.

But not everyone perceives becoming older as beautiful, or normal.

That's where ageism comes from.

Ageism is when *younger* grownups act unfairly to *older* grownups because of their age.

Ageism is possible when younger grownups have the power to make decisions for older grownups, such as where they live.

Kids and even other older grownups can act unfairly to older grownups, too. It's a form of **discrimination**, but ageism is a bit more specific.

Has someone ever made decisions for you that you wanted to make for yourself? How did that make you feel?

Ageism comes from thinking and feeling that growing older is bad.

Ageism is painful and hurtful.

Ageism is everywhere.

We've gotten so used to ageism that we may not notice it. **That's NOT OK!**

When we have the wrong idea about getting older, we may see aging as a problem. Or, be afraid of aging.

It wasn't always this way!

In the past, there was so much we learned from older grownups, and from connecting with people of all ages in our communities.

We do that less now. Why is that?

Now, we tend to value sources other than older grownups, turning to books or a quick internet search.

And we're constantly surrounded by messaging that tells us aging is bad.

Movies, advertisements, and stores spend a lot of money to make us think that being, feeling, and looking younger is always better than aging.

This has created **stereotypes*** about aging.

*A stereotype is an untrue belief that everyone in a group is the same.

Some stereotypes about older grownups include that they are ALL:

- Frail
- Dependent
- Useless
- Forgetful
- Slow
- Cute
- Grumpy

How do those words make you feel?

What words would you want people to use to describe you when you're much older?

What about all the incredible things that make each person who they are?

Ageism prevents people from sharing their talents.

Every one of us builds a beautiful, complex, important story as we age and grow.

So, how can you spot ageism? How can you stop it?

We're glad you asked!

It's important to know ageism happens in different ways:

**with ourselves,
with others,
and in groups.**

Ageism can stop older grownups from doing things they love because other people think it's not OK to do certain things once you're older.

Things like:

wearing certain clothes,

riding a bike,

dancing,

going to college,

working,

traveling,

being a parent,

or being in love.

Ageism can happen when we stereotype people by age group.

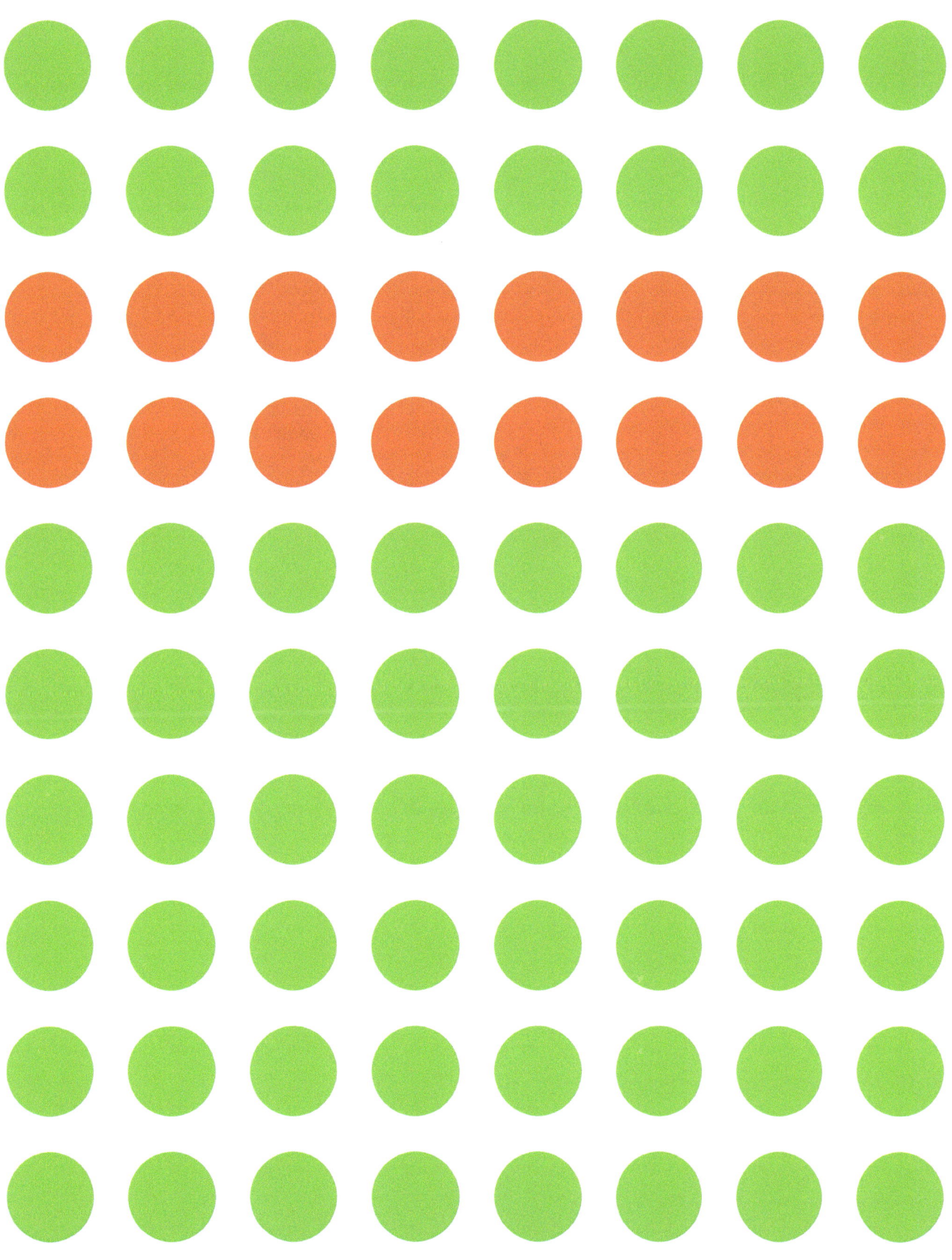

Are all kids under 18 the same?

Should all grownups over the age of 65 be treated the same?

Does that seem fair?

Ageism is everywhere,
and it happens all the time.

But it doesn't need to be the story that we keep telling ourselves.

All people are
valuable at

every age.

We have a new
story to tell when we...

think, feel, and act differently about aging.

When thinking and talking about aging and growing older, try adding these words to the discussion:

CAPABLE, RESILIENT, VIBRANT, CONNECTED, STRONG, FUN, SMART, KIND, DIVERSE, JOYFUL, CREATIVE, SEEN, INVOLVED, ACTIVE, SINCERE, BEAUTIFUL, GRACEFUL, AWARE, COMPASSIONATE, HELPFUL, ADAPTABLE, COURAGEOUS, WARM, LOVED.

Outro

Now that you've finished the book, we hope you see how strong our communities are when we include the contributions of older people—and everyone! We're stronger when we all belong.

Ageism has become culturally normalized and largely invisible. Now that you know about it, we hope you'll help others see it too. Together, we can tell a more complete story of aging. We need to arrive at a new understanding of ourselves and others that transcends age and ability, while still celebrating how those identities shape us. It's important to integrate aging, dementia, and disability into broader diversity, equity, and inclusion work.

Thanks for reading with us! We hope you'll help celebrate every age, and every ability.

About The Author

The Connecticut Age Well Collaborative fosters livable communities where we can all thrive across our lifespan. Core to our work is asking, what comes to mind when we hear words like "aging," "dementia," and "disability"? And how can we tell a more complete story about our changing minds and bodies?

The Collaborative's director, Alyssa Norwood, is a social entrepreneur, policy expert, attorney, and end-of-life doula, collaborating and connecting to promote inclusivity across the lifespan.

Lisa Rampulla Bress, Teresa Gregory Hines, and Cynthia Hyland are alumni of the Collaborative's Community Leaders Fellowship, which works to elevate the value of lived experience and build community authority.

Additional contributors are Christina Gray, Karen Green, Lesley Holford, and Julia Evans Starr.

 @ctagewellcoll    @ctagewellcoll    @ctagewellcoll

 ctagewell@ctcommunitycare.org

  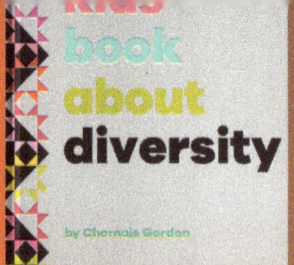  

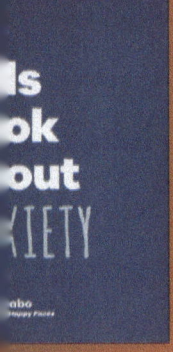 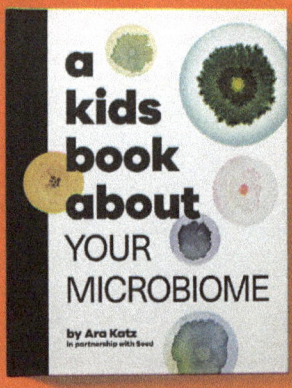   

Discover more at akidsco.com

www.ingramcontent.com/pod-product-compliance
Lightning Source LLC
Chambersburg PA
CBHW061358010526
44107CB00012B/981